# The Long Moment

KATE FAGAN was born in 1973 and lives in Sydney. She has published a short collection of poems, *return to a new physics*, and her poetry appears in *Calyx: 30 Contemporary Australian Poets*. Kate is the managing editor of *HOW2*, a US-based journal of innovative contemporary and modernist writing by women. Also a musician, she has performed extensively across Australia and in the UK.

Also by Kate Fagan

*return to a new physics*

# The Long Moment

## Kate Fagan

PUBLISHED BY SALT PUBLISHING
PO Box 202, Applecross, Western Australia 6153
PO Box 937, Great Wilbraham, Cambridge PDO CB1 5JX United Kingdom

All rights reserved

© Kate Fagan, 2002

The right of Kate Fagan to be identified as the
author of this work has been asserted by her in accordance
with Section 77 of the Copyright, Designs and Patents Act 1988.

This book is in copyright. Subject to statutory exception
and to provisions of relevant collective licensing agreements,
no reproduction of any part may take place without the written
permission of Salt Publishing.

First published 2002

Printed and bound in the United Kingdom by Lightning Source

Typeset in Swift 9.5 / 13

*This book is sold subject to the conditions that it shall not,
by way of trade or otherwise, be lent, re-sold, hired out,
or otherwise circulated without the publisher's prior consent
in any form of binding or cover other than that in which
it is published and without a similar condition including this
condition being imposed on the subsequent purchaser.*

ISBN 1 876857 39 0 paperback

SP

for Margaret & Bob & James
*altering the local song*

Contents

| | | |
|---|---|---|
| I | Calendar | 1 |
| II | return to a new physics | 13 |
| III | Anti-landscape | 51 |
| | Anti-landscape: lighthouse beach | 53 |
| | Lighthouse series | 56 |
| | 'Geophilosophy' | 66 |
| | Ecologue | 69 |
| IV | The waste of tongues | 77 |
| | The phoenix cup | 79 |
| | Being as such (eulogy) | 81 |
| | In pursuit of blue | 83 |
| | Sentience | 85 |
| | The waste of tongues | 89 |

## Acknowledgements

Thank you to the editors of the following journals and publications, for their encouragement and generosity in printing versions of some of these poems: *Calyx: 30 Contemporary Australian Poets*, *Famous Reporter*, *Five Bells*, *Jacket*, *Meanjin*, *Overland*, Poetryetc New Poetry Series, *Salt*, *Slope*, *Southerly*, *The Literary Review*, *The Prague Revue*, Vagabond Rare Object Series.

Special thanks to John Kinsella, Chris Hamilton-Emery and Salt Publishing for making this volume possible. Thanks also to Lyn Hejinian; to Pam Brown; to Kevin Hart; to Miranda Heckenberg; to Clive Newman; to Roslyn Oxley and the Roslyn Oxley9 Gallery in Sydney; and especially to the Gascoigne family, for kind permission to reproduce Rosalie Gascoigne's *Hung Fire*.

Finally and essentially, thank you to my family, first and constant real horizons. Unqualified thanks to Bergen O'Brien. Thank you to many lovely friends, especially to Kirsten Anker, Nancy Kerr and Alison Rawling. And thanks, in all ways, to Peter Minter.

Set it beside a tree, draw the road with chalk
and on the margins put *exit*.

I Calendar

# (april)

Against a grey sky thought appears differently, drowning in soapiness. A handful of change connects my hearing to a remnant of technological presencing. Something unutterable comes to rest between two morning letters. As soon as you begin the low walk down collapsing wooden stairs, a lens is directed to record a sense of purpose and I am startled at what returns, weeks later, in a quieter metropolis. Tulips and their messy gravity remember a thing previously imagined, now actualised. A shared vocabulary, that mechanical and cellular recognition. Cars glint almost charmingly along the river. Buildings have their impressive disregard for sound. Everything happens because of this chance encounter, a series of circles a street sign a long pavement or music wrapping into branches, apertures of air. Falling up adjunctive steps into a second scene. The future is just the future, starting yesterday.

# (may)

Twenty birds announce the difference, peculiar in their proximity to a recovered industrial dumping ground, peripheral pattern of this renewed attention to unfamiliar and impossible detail. Red cloth, then black. Walking to keep width in our faces as vertigo delivers us from each articulate second. Outside the café rolled bolts of printed cotton clock a particular shade of endlessness. We start to lose track of old rituals, aware of how things might arrive later. A deep and verdant ellipse, offered precisely. Breath becomes a figure of meeting. Beside water a thousand bright words hum into being, regional, translucent. What revelation, folding up a day. Cursive lines in a generous palm, green restaurant a clear signifier on an opening map, letters' flight meeting an alphabet. The bridge and its drifting wheel of gulls. Bodies strewn along the wharves, reflections too close to name, beginning to decide again.

# (june)

Coded eventualities, we throw handfuls of syntax and desire a kind of persuasive clarity, obviously mythic. The street becomes a conduit for breakages. Everyone I know appears there. Winter holding a pleasure of light, an absent lover, the absorbing difficulty of an ethics. At the corners of sight a corrugated fence clicks in a breeze, particular to this description. Meticulous print, excoriation, eruptions of wild possibility making sharp turns toward desperation in care. At times we are more present in writing. There is that in poetry, the sound of a great improvisation. Coffee splits the distance between us over and over. Three points of colour visible from the small window beside the bath, announcing continuity. Each day proliferate with things eluding trace. We all begin to share a body memory of forgetting, noise in a cloudy margin, persistent and entomological.
I carefully arrange songs and imagine a rapid flight out.

## (july)

Holding hands we leap off jagged rocks for a video camera, not needing to communicate our knowledge of why. It will only move forward in disattached places. Calendula, a blue jug, candles and punctual smoke, the slow fret of uneven talk. I reappear with space in my gestures and gather a few things, turning back to gaze along the coastline. Each shudder of metal cites a dark evolution, wallaby ghosting as light drains into a road of gums, one frantic possibility. Indifferent rain buckets down between great washes of sea. We stride toward freesias with the narcissistic joy of equally-matched heights. Shadow of irises, exquisite scapula, angelic pitch in a room of temporary dust, arms out beside the fence, beams as spokes of a giant circus, purple evening, details we might wish for later. The crescent moon patiently regarding haphazard sand. A whale, a star, two names for a present child, twinning temporalities, every return measured against this one.

(august)

Emptying over a balcony, slow light recalls the loss of a city.
The word and repeatedly. Saltiness scalds. Perhaps this is the life
we have dreamed, close beside bone. We are unafraid to touch it
for a blue second and this passes for miraculous. Hugging our
skin on cooling concrete, distraught with trying to tell how.
Single gulls edge aside crows. At the far limits of corporeal
certainty, held in water, hearing water. Gifts are passed across an
increasingly ragged membrane, a cup, a feather, an idea, a poem.
Under my hands one-and-a-half thousand days seem to melt
alarmingly, the visceral reach of sorrow. Each of them requires
patient testing. Red stature angled to the leaning zone,
escarpment of night, a halo leaking through the stratosphere.
Though determined to find another language for it, we reiterate
certain learnt narratives. Familiar saxophone glancing off
the midnight walls of central tunnel, quiet windows, a phone
number jammed in among coins.

(september)

In a secondhand shop I find obscure printed validations of these fledgling connective practices and hope again for excess. One fold words into another. Art is rescued near the slowly expanding garden. The second spring returns memory but we are wearing different things. Melbourne fragments arranged carefully, a promise of vodka, your lipstick night, oranges and light words, a singular red bead. Summoning energy for another magic trick, inversion of capabilities, language threading the hours. On the town hall steps holding photographs of patina-bright blocks, scattered not far from the colour field. Crowding in to witness philosophy, a leaving, long translucent petals. People crane to hear your lines tumbled as whispers, itching to be associated. Curiosity translates metonymically. Some relations are improbable, some are inevitable. I walk out to a second lighthouse carrying nothing and fall sideways as the wind dumps ocean onto our arms, preserving us.

(october)

Muted trumpet absorbed by a cold watching dam, scratchiness of nights without intimacy. The gap between expectation and eventuality. A stunning cerise, long clouds turn between rows of glassy leaves. Nothing but the difference. A flash of breakfast on Bourke St, a room glimmers, utterly you say. Already things are receding. There are weeks where nothing happens but the memory of other weeks, a pub near the hospital, contesting forms as evacuated shells, this quiet appreciation. Meticulous jointed mornings. We can't say for sure what will not occur. Exact rounds of lotus, floating downhill. Events outstrip our worded attempts to arrest them. A novel applauded, gathering in respectful circles to provoke and reminisce, departure like the sun. The smallest actions return storms of consequence. Declarations hold. Arriving to burn written joy on the doorstep, trust stemming, displacement repetitive and indelibly historical.

(november)

Skin emergent as silence, lightly crossing territories. A plane flying east from the horizon becomes a vaporous comet. Humming vista, inky sincerity, we begin to miss the future as well. Something unutterable comes to rest between two morning letters. Swinging against groundlessness, cautiously declared. You wake from a calm dream of impossibly tall forests. Desire separates, reforms along the diagonals of a meshed steel frame. Hyperrealism arranged in parataxis. Sharp coriander, its immaculate perimeters. It is accepted that no story has a beginning, a middle or an end. Three floors of a warehouse shaken with traffic. A history of pages flung into air, patterning the shift. Our speech starts to reinterpret mathematics as we sink into artificially warm water. Mah-jong tiles fluttering against a lengthening seam. Sculptures are visible in the distance, elegant and superfluous, as we bite our tongues.

(december)

Where hail has broken the vast roof a galaxy of stars hangs, noticeable only by day. Deliberately edged and remaining here. A red sign scripting water. Each affirmation of detail is a tracking of context made new. Two eggs spinning in a deep blue bowl. Carefully segmenting an orange, citric astringency beside sweet black tea, your voice fantastically evaporative. Leaning my head back against a round mirror, I reimagine a small white horse, then Permian cacti, then one fluorescent stem. We search for different forms and promise different habitats. Enumerating predictions, all of them useless. The smell of your hair remaining on my hands. Two raw scars, scraps of torn paper on either side of a caressed spine, intellect's light intent. We continue to occupy this world, it appears in erratic scrawls, patient and actual. Where nothing refers to nothing.

II  return to a new physics

beside ourselves
we wait for light
and arrange lake things
spectating upon the inevitable

this breath pulls apart a dandelion
with related intensity
seed-heads
springing into maps

leaving speed
to other equations and valencies,
we are splitting prisms
hoping
for slow fantastic
disturbance

and pointing at nothing
as it empties

tricking the vena cava,
beginning to measure
a thing near blood's bright flow

what isn't used
to distortion

i slip along an eyelash
in a curious
repeating crawl,
taking notice
of intimacy's accompaniments

respecting machinery
and the way component cogs
tender their own music,
the task
apparently
is to be more than cellular

one needle of light
breaks this face
planar sharply
and unintentional

at an eye,
a performance of shading
demands
graceful attention

unblinking,
temporality crystallizes

here perception renders
prior choices irrelevant
consequence
sliding down blank

dipping and translucent
mapping our regional

crossing flowers,
a morning becomes
instantly red and yellow
a trade of
perfectly animate matter

what is it about narcissism
that suggests
only deserved loss as an option,
when detailing the space
of conflict
is possible
and exquisite?

saluting air,
contesting vacancy,
we sift and pull among
calm strings of zeros

each syllable
a vector
an atomic spatial practice

we concern ourselves
with the most tender evidence
of specificity

quantum materials
showing in waves
with properties at the level of light

our units of significance
are shrinking
and in doing so,
upset scale irretrievably

this is not about visibility
one rhetorical grid placing
fragment after fragment

we step into locations
and change them, or they
happen to us

this tries to acknowledge
a hazardous story
of occupation

as night fell over the hill
or a leaf startled
it became apparent
that the vista
would reinterpret us

space incremental,
collecting in events

the sheer height of the harbour
or the way one light
offered a series and clairvoyance

a clear mode of measurement
and responsibility
might present,

looking for angelic reason
or accuracy

muscle tissues cleave,
twist as
copper-sexed lizards
i lay on the concrete
wondering if this was any way
to think like a reptile

a choice
to augment corporeality,
restoring a politic
to certain systems
and embodiments

you gaze across a window,
feeling interiors crowd
or dismantle

an impossible window
with numberless starts
the way
our shadows
refuse consolidation

i am enticed
by these penumbrae
their questions
inviting in
morality and movement

a world walking around
open-mouthed
and collapsing

who does futurity
share itself with

agency is bleakly comical
in some scenarios
or beyond economy

in serious rituals
and relative
language,

we receive and return
movement,
choosing how
to dance the problem
of space

at its most optimistic
and devastating
this might alter the local song

rhetoric is addictive
circumstantially
a possible effect
of aesthetics in welcome crisis

something molten,
practical
or cumulative,
carnivals of talk
immeasurably precise
as quicklime

we time light
in heliographic intervals
interrogating display, message,
apparatus, sense

this process seems more significant
than looking at the sun

so a river repeats,
one narrative
of urbanite *getaway*,
water in service
to monotony's break

or a paddock
ghosted
by seemly gums
language squint
and referring

lyric interjects
demanding specific
impatient approval

quick like junk,
memorial about position
and meaning

i sort among
memories' allowances
to distinguish sameness from recognition

the way a knee
fits into the back of another,
a hand curling
briefly around a cup
to arrest its spill,
eucalyptus barkfall
in cracking strips

what kind of artificial nature
is this
infinitely repeatable
prized and cultural
the local avoiding
sentimental anecdote

letters' flight
meeting distance
& an alphabet,

*a sheaf of measure*
*against what slips,*

these patient offerings
to memory

our hands settle
around great resonant
stomachs,
disharmonic
with sound

what body
knows consistency,
pleated
in sense

the effort gathered in
one digit, navigating one dense
region of skin

this sensuality
resides in mobile boundaries

take off your body
accretive, porous, speckled
against imperious narrations
about perceivable objectivity
or becoming by

a creased lid
yesterday's struggle over syntax
untidy veins
until grass emerges
or moss edges between,
complex as water

then numbers accumulate,
seasonal,
in sure steps

the way parting
divides rooms
or folds in silently

*i* swings against
evening's yellow grey
choosing
this phrase
that exact expressive footfall
as it thuds
to road

sound evaporative,
motion in the first instance
blurring

it was impossible
to know this
as distinct history

coordinates fly
into language,
air bleeding
and excited
in overnight winds
that elongate

glancing aside
to where regard
has thickened

becoming occupied,
a prescient snatch of song,
a missed poem
blinking offscreen

try to address
the entire situation
that a person presents,
distributing context

placement falls under suspicion
like landscape

culture might become useful
in this torque
of perception

when colonisation
is relegated to tropes
of prior authenticity
and post white-confession,
something like preterite babble
is resurrected
to violate

we recover plates
thickening with sight,
with desire,
history's
worn cadence

are you troubled
by erasure
do you drink
to compulsion

a guarding
chemical blur,
stories proximate
and disfigured

uneven silver links,
this impetus to record,
to find place

this is not epic
but serial
who needs another hero

dusk
and its vagaries
afford desire
local options

littered among walls,
under morphemes,
this, aside and
mechanical
but breaking

the way
or shifting

pleasure and performative
unscene

a person distrusts poetry
it didn't function
as expected

between imaginaries
and what arrives
or passes,
vertigo smiles
a dizzying smile

locale shifts
around a clock,
reputedly different
at each hand

a sun shimmers
how to distinguish time
trees' whisper a fiction
pixellated and scenic

a thousand sentences
near optimism

between you or i,
aspirate
and consonant,
an otherworld
gets to appear

smatterings of percept
collect,
well worded
and situate
this nowhere

bumping
along the lie
of utopia's text
its measure of ending

vocabularies segue,
rills in coincidence
or radical transfer

recuperating care
from possible misadventure

you occupy the hyphens
distracted by sense
and departure

what can tide you over,
bending to collect
a point here,
a shift there,
cast-offs
rendered sane
with longing
in the arrest of loss

particular to texture
the way silver
skims at your hair

or three pores,
inky with melanin,
align

conversation appears
to mist the table top,
dragged
under a sleeve

ecstatic about repair
and memory,
comedy's devices

laughing at shocking
theme-music
and mouthing complicity

irreplaceable as reason
a sense of the life
whole and between

i startle,
your yelp
for nascence
a bright, lonely rendition
of familiarities' wake

pointillistic love
unmistaken
in its reliance
on skin, element,
shard matter

the changing sorrows
of space
and sound

high tin corrugations
scored at angle
by low winter light
and curving

afternoon slows
in a series
of spatial shifts
disturbing chrono-logic

an instant
gusty and canvas,
heat across the elliptical table,
a word thrown
at passing wheels

*inimitable wind*
i write again,
signifying nothing sharp

or from this eye
to there
the peripheral catch
of wind
rocking wire

a shadow
redistributes,
becomes the impact
of autumn's way
of moving things

how to distinguish
sight from perception

leaning into description
pulling on letters
as they shift,
attuning eyes' work

you experience again
a room as synaesthesia,

arrangements of shade
introduce an ear
to music
or to seeing

i recall the way
one woman
perpetuates
as a certain moment
of walking through a cityside park

smoke roughens,
we misremember gestures,
the sense of sleeping
clearly, or of place
disappearing

after dark
implies morning

or interior occasions
when things receive
memory's outline

different how,
a day perceived
and textured
by night,

and yesterday's
bright occurrence
returned in this
diurnal language

deft hours, kind ecstasy,
writing the object
or its circumstance

what approaches
immaculate indivision

there is nothing

we tease apart a rain
of spectra
cast in sentences,
each spit of matter
volatile, capable

pressing into a day's
peculiar gravity

in response to queries
about sincerity,
the text
patiently accretive

arranging scorched wrists, breath,
sweet morning, echo, ambivalence

and this
coruscation
close to knowledge
what else
can it offer

sky's break
over distance
puzzling clouds
version after version
of between and blue

a record for the living,
notice pinned
to detail,
observation and dream
cognisant
of light's change

here morning
is another inquiry
our body
waiting to happen

suspicious about placement
but not unhappily

i find this elegant

your hand's move
in rearranging
dust motes
on one quiet sleeve,
consequential

or how loose hair
eddies at a corner
with each absenting
and arrival

rain's insistence
silvers a street
their clear lake

room to room
we collide,
they close behind us,
into another
ritualised mode,
specific and comic

clear *in the sense
of silence*

the thing
that recognises dying
flies off a word,
burns
with happening

superfluity
present elation

near a tilting bridge
a crowd
moving over
my bodies'
skew compositions

even,
openly

graffiti bawls
at each extremity

lips' density
uncertain,
words accident,
sitar limns
a high window

*precession* the
slow movement
of the axis
of a spinning body

around another axis
*precession of*
*the equinoxes*
1 the slow

retrograde motion
of equinoctial points
along the ecliptic
2 the resulting

earlier occurrence
of equinoxes
in each successive
sidereal year

*& each time the moment falls*
*the emphasis of the moment falls*
*into time differently*

continued presencing
if not the present

these caring accretions,
*the life that has gone*
acknowledged
as detail,
repeating in place

each time the tongue moves
it moves into time differently

doing, undoing
a bundle of precisely-wired blue
& this & this
appearing

# III Anti-landscape

## Anti-landscape: lighthouse beach

You are walking among ribs,
waking

each skeleton composed to the height
of a hand

falling upward into sky,
into grace,

ocean's caress a touch
lighter than history,

arrives as history,

exacting and dense and drifting sand
away from these

unconcealed remnants,
timely exposures

beached and collected in gestures
of appalled compassion


We remark that this stretch of land could write us eternally

For a moment only sand-light burying hands
are out of place,

each mattered thing
with its own belonging

then echoing
along a wasted track, association

of metal castings, an idea made machine
and coming ashore

driven ashore

claiming usefulness,
asserting watchfully-anxious imperial certainty


Our choice
encounters us

as one broken commodity after another,
plastic bottles and bags

heaped against styrofoam irrelevancies


Written or unwritten, the details collect and return us to context

Your light picks out the convex thought
of an eye,

ear heart tail ghosting,
a dog following the fishing,

your tired whistle into territory to externalise breath,

to sound what you sense is not unspeakable
but finely-tuned,

balanced or hung at an ecological edge


Salt tangle of drying grass
measures the wind,

then the coded dune,

patterns the shift as it does

## Lighthouse series

Evolving map
spitting up a whale, dragged skein of a whale,
each current of hide or fin,

material density.
This and this step sinking,
unit of interference approaching a boundary

assembled in wash, blubber, observation,
folding silica, seaplant stem beside.
Cell decay, now regenerate

lingers on a hand attentive to bone jag,
unable to gouge
a twisted molar cavity,

quiet desecration perplexing.
From every point on a sand crescent
a remnant worded, punctual as light.

Curious gravity of mouths
or situated longing, the way corporeality
attaches to happening detail. Tooth

grinding sand, this planar sweep of rib
a carapace, invert. Tongues break
between edges,

cross tides, reeling in place.
The dune looks back
scrambling and wintered.

Sideways light handful of sand
clouds to a breeze,
striated, shimming part

and part, eventually submerged
as information
licking & saline & written.

Vanishing form again, zeros
start up in surprise.
Or a table of sun, dragging

at my arms, a cast,
a way of responding to weather's gift.
Screen door enters. A music

of occurrence or one thought
punctuated & met by shore,
breath, prismatic

and exquisite. Shift as it does.
A scene happens and moves me
off a mote of regard

without anxiety. Stars of green
strung light to a stem,
convolvulate, strophic.

Cast iron rail leans to uncertain
height. Measured filament
glows in a repeating lens,

song's quiet machine keeping
light's motion perpetual,
heard in syntax.

One hundred thousand candelas,
one hundred thousand shadows' grace
framed in a moment,

this mathematical ekstasy
turning skyward. Combine,
recombine at interval,

evening's clear cerulean
gives appearance to inky night,
happens to perception.

Cartographies of belly and spine,
moray hide flecking
out of fingered transit,

clasping vocabularies' exactness
to cervices' end.
Sea peal interrupts,

ghostly, to change the tone.
What laughs through windows or lets us see.
Or moves this, organic

& angular, out to another tide,
strewn around us
leaking, nothing existing

in the distance. Breathing through your throat
to where hip bones protrude, your gravity
at appropriate extremes.

We begin where we can in one language
and shift to another,
& another, &

a day when nothing
looks backward or forward,
mon espoir. Expecting to italicize

in blueing sun, the way an aroma
eats this plane between neck and lobe,
attentive, radicalized

and stretching as lawn
to fence's hold over gusty spray,
vertigo in check for a moment.

Half buried cleated skull
and lower jaw of a seabird,
towing out the rain.

Our dervish light at sky's edge,
fresh waters disperse
in silicic creases, lost sound drop

-ping from a jet, quiet arch.
Significant rain skews history,
chisels an embankment,

a new cirque. This fret about ecologies.
Characters' trace between s& dollars,
sight, a person, a harbour

providing our lingua franca,
handfuls of commas attesting
truth to context as *slow and silent*

*these bodies enact*
*their mutual abandonment*
, this & that unhinged, afloat.

Everything about to happen, turning
& windowed by this attention.
One yellow corolla

a measure of resistance
to loss, to another's loss,
to a thing slipping

in cellular time. So
we attach this worded regard
to an instant,

recreating immediacy.
What leans into form,
our perception of thick matter,

translucent coin of olive oil
nudging at a glazed edge
and promising relief.

Memory, saturate until the membrane
will admit nothing more.
The system shifts &

we listen to what passes
to,  from,  a hand at a rim,
a concept folding or unfolding,

the wide interval
between your ankles.
A story about light retells us.

Beside the lookout path,
the last to catch sun,
& moving toward movement,

a patient dog is not a figure
of constancy. We are unconcerned
about how to dream, just that it does.

Again, speaking this present
and its rapid drift into distance,
proximate time spilt

among tenses. We acknowledge
how a moment moves
to local completion. You say

what is the moment. Adjusting scale
for each print, gesture or thing
pressed in as texture,

repeating later in a photograph
or letter, quieter & looser.
Some details pass unarrested,

there is pleasure in forgetting.
Subjectivities cohere and melt.
Cloud as cloud is.

## 'Geophilosophy'

1

Winter drags itself slowly across the interval occupied by a thought of sky. When I lean to name them, clouds dissipate and suggest something else, felt as ineffable. Each conscious spark beside an increase of mattering, the mineral fact of pressing ourselves to the drying grass, the inevitability of our lips and their open gravity. The word *terrain* begins to unlock the perimeters of reason, returns a dream and watchfulness, everything resolves into a method of composure held in a geometry borrowed from trees. As if aquamarine, torn over by foam, collecting the wind, could become a way of thinking. A tiny insect, its abdomen sectioned into red and turquoise bands, wings askew beside the edge of vision, confirming the reach of a morning's desire. We let our eyes empty into sand, tensile, replete in care, spray hurled at forty-five degrees along one prismatic face of interruptive rock. Every clod, nerve fibre, branching stem or netted radical offers an idea of earth memory. Our seagull voices shrieking to the ridge, I am only the stretch of your arms holding there, nothing to defy, cellular abrasion or the entry of salt water licking at a membrane. Eagles wheel up, a message of clear territory, seen by them, I witness your *déjà vu* or bird-becoming and reach out with charcoal on my fingers to respond again, leaving a trace on your forehead that lasts only as long as the drafted space between breaths. Green algae thrown to beach beside tender blue and silver fish, ideas of their beginning, evolute collisions marked in by footprints. Affinities, learnt within these dense material systems, an immaculate bone replicates an entire submerged body or a path picked out over cliffs. We hope to abandon possession, rinse in scars. Nothing incorporeal, nothing without linkage, sounding a different scale of regard. *The landscape is a somatic discourse*, habitus is disarranged. Another tide moves, right to this shore, red clay appears just as a squall folds in off a steel horizon and your heels find a point of balance, embedded. Language in extreme generation, all scenes saturate in story, shouldn't we behave as this, decide to uncouple from closing, and how? Cytoplasms under scrutiny, asking in weather, uttering a rhythm of surroundings in pure and impure movement.

2

Stem
*un*lock territ-
               ories

besides
repainting the ledge,

*dusting out words until*
        *with barely*
               *line or two,*         the core of
    *a vaster, -existent*

in disarray, tactile
        as geometry

borrowed from
trees
               a fact    compassing

*y/our* belly along grass,

                                                *stolen*

lasting
im-pressures    *algal spatter*
scripting a beach,

                         *wrecked along the coast*

stone appurtenance
               this perpendicular        light vantage

slow recovery of
          *discoursing*
   all bound,

(return to left
margin

*cellular abrasion or the entry of salt water*
                             *licking at a membrane.*

# Ecologue

As if in burial country
where all interlopers and tourists
shift with immersion, something exposed,
a precondition for history


Spitting into density,
thick beaching crops of spinifex,
permission to wander, no boundary
without an opening


A common stranding place
for minke whales, skeletal signs
appear overnight in rain, skin macabre,
rots in sanded découpage

Language of a microcosm
heard in layers, ritualised by efforts
of filmic capture, a system
bent by intrusion


Messy subtleties
atomised into code, lysis
at a shoreline, skimming beside
surfaces of ruined rock


The sand is grey
where oil seeps from stone,
a passer-by yearns for insides, replaces
one face with another

And in the kitchen, overland wires down,
a gale howling at the bell, each
resonant clang sounding
a lie of centuries


Shiplight gloss pulled
over wave toward wave as sand
flies out of the winding second, calamity
might arrive again


Twists of iron buttressing
the curving rail, marked by rust,
holding the loss of architecture at bay,
preserve of a cautious few

One broken body
cast up, thin with breath
and narration, etched into
a wall of cells


Collapsed tracks were
a site of entry for steel,
following a previous invasion
to bring an idea of light


The detail evolute,
for a moment there is no field,
background not surreal but hyperreal:
our history of displacing

Each branch remembers
abstract time, supporting thought,
bark shifts through
formal cacophony


A sinker slips in foam,
point of carnal interface, mapped
against the liquid undertow
of purpose


Indifferent figures
wave toward an exit,
renewal demands
a difficult inscription

Desecration is a sharp
and brilliant beam, splitting
each rotation to usher in
complex removal


Roughened squares,
lineations of skin at the crest
of another dune, configuring
a modal present


Sunbleached carcass
buried for an endless age
by slow-lettered sand, miracle
of anatomism

Landscape is undone,
our structural safety zone,
static intentions exposed
between names


Royal stamp
affixed to the engine,
a fine imperial machine
turning at the governor's pleasure


Stark at a surface,
palimpsest of parched earth
ordered in dramatic
archaeology

Uneasy leaden reach of silt
sculptural and saline,
clavicular trace beside
littered polymers


A freeze, fumbling for location,
theatrical remnants in coastal towns,
sharpening the tongue,
leaving quietly


Imprint: from a dream before,
keeping careful measure
of erasure, even so,
sounding this disturbance

# IV  The waste of tongues

# The phoenix cup

Even the sky
cannot convince us
of its perimeters,

that bright recovery of space
hung to a word,
counterfeiting vision,

today's syntactical comforts
thinning out
under pressure

of branches
broken into petal,
dissembling as always

August slips by
in a quiet, borderless exercise
of syringes and mercurial investigations,

sense rusting at my fingertips
and dropping in flakes
to a bleached floor

Here is later,
arranged so that the sun
might know us,

what is offered
held for a moment in something
we term recognition,

blood leaching to tissue
as unforgotten sap
from relinquished soil

Our rooms are crowded with rituals,
unhurried calls
smudging the distance

and tacking down
*the canvas of this night*,
incessant numbering,

a generous attachment
to found objects,
sexual certainties in skin,

the fiery leap
of breakage
and careful readherence

Our poems
currawong their way
through our actual world,

each opalescent minute
picked and sounded,
perpetual departure in echo

## Being as such (eulogy)
*for K.J.R.F.*

Falling outside the lower limit
of another's wild speech,

a sentence pronounces itself
without walls or eyes
but with music

This embarkation and offering

Materially bound
and starred to a hill of indeterminate frost,
open beside windows of quiet salt,

we embrace first as cells
the sorry loss of a fine jawbone,
then change
in its finer reasoning

Other near objects
are craved as we crave seeing
to arrange descriptions of spirit,

unmovable sun
leaking into intervals of consciousness,

dust at an abandoned spine,
drops as pleased as summer
gathered by a dissolving fenceline

It's not for nothing that we inquire
though not
for knowledge either,

our 'best lines'
receding as they borrow
enough history to move sideways
with a practical awareness of the lightness of longevity,

its relative absence on a scale
of presencing

If fortunate we witness agonal inhalations
as though cleanly chosen
and, where protected,
maintain a sweet longing
to close the distance between our souls
and our carnal, ordinary dilemmas

A useful sentence
collects the time,
spaces the events of thinking,
our accidental place among leaves

## In pursuit of blue

Numb on our parallel
we throw silence
at the sky,

pull drunken rain
down over us,
remember

an acute haze
of vowel sounds
and left-over possibles

Nothing as sparse
as breathing,
nothing as particular

Bent on a back porch
counting leaves
and unquiet stars,

a chance arrival of strings
and polaroid blues
We reach to a sea floor,

climb wet
with a smooth chunk
of ocean in our hands,

surprising and licked
as the word
*turquoise*

You trace along a map
to show me
how many red dirt roads

we can fit
between our torn lips
and cracking breastbones

At this point
and this, we stop
to admire the sudden view,

the way ordinary angels
make up the score
of comforts

that pin us
to the movable earth,
carried high

on stories,
a bright catalogue
of emotional graces

We fold up
this understanding
and mortal sense,

pack it quickly
into two cases
and split the difference

# Sentience

1

this sound breath makes

crossing between bright suggestion and skin
stretched to our historical backs, arms along pearling thigh to edge
    resounding in agile matter,
its porous, gleaming density audible
    as wave after cornered wave of precise sky,

tucking ourselves into each fold or limit,
    a lifting of bone to meet bone over the long reach of a sentence,
an idea, spectacular division of lust
emerging later as light

2

what seduction a tongue might exert

as a story gently topples one chord against another dripping
    fine subject into subject,
placing necks, a sense of sudden visibility drags an eye
from point to point,

slow,
read and interpret erotic scenery

as some thing brushing one syllable up along the ridge of a lip,
    spilling to gather
whatever then becomes a detail revisiting, hardly heard
in the arrest of seconds

3

clear and leaning into attention

face limning flesh as form
glances into split composure and remains alert
    sucking on air,
its quick imprint, what then appears as cobalt, flies

beside thought and this increase of arrival,
    transmutes as desire,
the remembered dance of a thousand jagged pieces,
    deferral an excess of touch a cry sustaining the social,

imagines sex
    offered in word display,
dissociates and returns in other tellings

4
bitten between limb,

belly,
    and whatever number of stars
become constellations of circumstance in wild address, turning back
to laugh loudly
    at insides rendered outer

    while evenly demanding
that this mess embrace itself as morning's immediate action,
touching each perimeter
    and certain as teeth in eating space
over and over,

a horizon of intimate syllables,

one measured evolution of grace waxing on skin
or a red sign scripting water

## The waste of tongues

It is impossible to stand on an ice-cube
in the right way. There is a permeable membrane
between evening sky and evening star. You take
a favourite pen and write 'relativity' in neat cursive
somewhere in the unempty zone of a fresh page,
watching the way your *i* has changed over time,
a swift equation forming, $i\,/\,$time. There's a
*down-to-the-wire count* on a well-tuned radio
for the new president, two hard halves falling
open on a desk, a choice of monosyllables.

While a clock hauls itself over the four, our faces
bump as mothwings under looping arcs of light
let in above a torn block-printed curtain. I am
about to speak of nightmares but don't know this yet.
A man who has 'returned' catapults every day
past the front window, shouting a quiet shout
to the pavement, watching the way anxious people
herd their children to the street's developed other kerb
on pretence of a walk in the sun. Hilary Clinton
wins New York on a tilt of the word *we*.

One moment's *entre* when bamboo leaves
float in a bath in late afternoon. A hand, reaching
into the hollow of my chest, winged by folded ribs,
would find a sound of whole glass bubbles. You
are searching for the distance between here
and now. The ink dries at a point where or when
perception moulds unmoving objects from the paste
of process. Meanwhile, pirates take a tanker
in the open waters, ladders quickly up the side,
silent paint, a different name.

There is no end to geometry, the crisp terrain
of triangles your arm marks out across
my lip. Arable and floating, the gentle lake
that pools along your sternum. Syntax, sharp
as something that cannot be held, and therefore
loud as the slip away from tactile certainty.
In the earth, still with flight, sleeping bodies hum
intemporal distrust. Beside them, we are counting
memes, how love makes up for death. *You mean
that's your idea of desire, with all those commas?*

Penumbral at the island of a camera's
second eye, you are less than disconcerted,
more than disaffected. Strings of numbers thread
the seconds, our talk is patterned with absurdities,
shopping lists in hypertext. This could be
democracy boulevard, though the clothes are
too expensive, the seams still faintly warm
and loose. Song lyrics unfold in neon,
incredulous in a third language, *who is where
on the planet?* Six miles out a robot circles Eros.

A fan of poems is a trumped-up hand of cards,
nostalgic by-ways and bucket loads of sentiment,
engagement brooks a brimming chest of hope.
One writes the index entries and another
checks the list with perfect ticks. That should read,
perfect texts. A turn around the culture bureau,
papers that are left on show. Nearby, a corridor
is yellow with the smell of roasting cinnamon,
oil smoulders in its second use, closer to
one heart of things, further from others.

Tall printed ships arrive, light sails swing
from exacting masts, this splintered ante-arctic
breath. A word—*balcony*—begins to curl
at my mind's tongue, tectorial seduction
of a lexeme, one licked syllable against another,
delayed delay, *salut*. Rains arrive, the Tees
is flooding, carrying to mouth the burnt detritus
of a steely present, a past of arches, bright
slaggy stacks of Long & Dorman broken
from the chain arms of exhausted apparatus.

You are asking, red over blue, about
artifice and its obliquities. Each deft scale
edges toward instauration. The lintel is given
to fortune's gift, a seam of coal, a radial bone
flung up to meet the kelpline, just, octaves
of chalk, consolations of a life arranged
in diatonic. What we think to hear within
'the broad sweeping form' of being there,
being here. Between the articles you say
that *teleos* is never less than myth.

A single ibis, curving *threskiornis*,
threads the clotted path from here to Mascot,
missing poles and planes. Several degrees fall
from a burning sky, sweep roadward
under anvil cloudheads. Does it surprise you,
this matter of voices? Or rather, the space
imagined for a cultural collision, argent bird
and ordered tree, elapsing as thought only.
Ecologies of type and temper sprawl to meet
the corners. *Look out, star walking.*

A clock for longitude, central to the talk
of empires, glassy face of contest between
artisans and royal star-gazers. This fetish
for cartographies, a legal key to desecration,
to the grinding trade. You wonder at a transit
of Venus, James Cook's superficial brief.
Isabell Coe claims Cockatoo Island, carries
healing smoke from fence to fence,
remembering a captain's terra scrawl
to plush seats at the court Supreme.

During the inauguration party, nobody
seems to mind as the new boss happily watches
twenty pairs of All-American legs, transfixed
or *Bedazzled*, while plotting the appointment
of a pro-protection team. He takes cues
from his father, who took cues from an actor,
and this is welcomed. An included middle
fills expansively with ghosts. Outgoing bodies
wave to a new centre left, rugged-up well
to meet intoxicating January ice.

Sixty miles clear of Gloucester, a person
stands beside a glass case, the promise
of stuffed charms, left hand holding coins
and right hand poised to anchor pink ducks
for love. POP 330, chipped paint
and retrospection hamburgers, satellites
to a year-old Supermall. Two flash lads
wear suits to the movies, one folds the other
into a cuff of his jacket, tenderly. *I am
the avant-garde and so is my wife.*

'Your heart is indebted to the life's
blood of my heart,' they read, alphabets
of serious romance. Electrolytic winds
carry a memory of memory. Define the way
fruit-fly make precise ampersands of scribble
on these ripening skins, the way spiders sing
to the weather's approach. A lion bends
its ankle to the step, shaking by a paperfall
of fireworks, red cut-ups for a new year.
Pocketful of genres, selected.

For a fortnight you speak to me
from the furthest lake, each encounter
along its glazed perimeter. Nothing is dusty
because everything is dust. Experience
in transposition, a memory sets firm without
indifference, a phone on the hill blinks
in and out as we hang from a satellite.
At the hotel bar you wonder who pays
for a silver and rose underworld, as though
when he said spectacular, he meant it.

Lucent bodies dare the velar ocean,
a watchful dog becomes the pacific distance.
When an eye meets another eye it knows
it has been sighted, just as a living body
knows the present absence of a lifeless one.
She said sometimes I envy the rhetoric
of devotional rituals, as contrails crossed
behind her in a pealing easter sky.
*Yea, though I walk through the valley*
*of the shadow of death, I will fear no evil.*

Spiking on jazz, hyaline and suave.
Vocabulary oils slip and refuse to dry.
Kyoto sets its clock to run permanently
backward. Strangeness enters quietly
to erase its own condition, sorrow
tastes of clouds, extinction in bronze.
A sense of deafness pulls my heels
to the road, covers my face. We sing
for shocks of difference, every code
abandoned in a rapture of technology.

*A writer cannot inherit an instance.*
To dwell in the arrangement of things,
an open line, equating mode with spirit.
Give me an anchor in all this space,
embed us. A full orange moon is cornered
by adjustable horizons, temporal as anything.
News that absorbs news, a language of care,
we want to touch the drifting matter
of its mattering, sweet reason in *this-topia*,
context and a mineral fact.

# Notes

*apertures of air* Arkadii Dragomoschenko

Lyn Hejinian *there is that in poetry, the approach of a great improvement*

*a sheaf of measure against what slips* Susan Howe

George Oppen *clarity in the sense of silence*

*and each time the moment falls it falls into time differently* Lyn Hejinian

Louis Zukofsky *the life that has gone*

*to begin in one language and end up in others* Joan Retallack

Tracy Ryan *slow and silent these bodies enact their mutual abandonment*

*geophilosophy* Gilles Deleuze and Félix Guattari

Arkadii Dragomoschenko *the landscape is a somatic discourse*

*tacking down the canvas of this night* Michael Ondaatje

Michael Palmer *you mean that's your idea of desire, with all those commas?*

*who is where on the planet?* Daniel Böniger

Kit Robinson *democracy boulevard*

*the broad sweeping form of being there* Joanne Kyger

Fanny Howe *the silver and rose underworld*

*shocks of difference* Lyn Hejinian

Logan Esdale *a writer cannot inherit an instance*

Epigraph from *Xenia* by Arkadii Dragomoschenko,
translated by Lyn Hejinian and Elena Balashova

*return to a new physics* written for Peter Minter in correspondence

'Ecologue' written in response to *Kangaroo Virus* by John Kinsella

www.ingramcontent.com/pod-product-compliance
Lightning Source LLC
Chambersburg PA
CBHW022106040426
42451CB00007B/154